MW01001306

MY PARTNER
Prayer Journal

BECKY TIRABASSI

OLIVER
NELSON
™

THOMAS NELSON PUBLISHERS®
Nashville

A Division of Thomas Nelson, Inc.
www.ThomasNelson.com

MY PARTNER
Prayer Journal

DATE_____

INTRODUCTION

My Partner Prayer Journal is a personal, *spiritual life* organizer that provides a place for you to:

- journal your prayers,
- record God's answers, and
- store inspirational teachings and studies.

In addition, *My Partner Prayer Journal* can become an accountability tool to help you:

- keep a daily appointment with God, and
- organize your prayers and Bible reading.

In 1984 my spiritual life was slowing to a halt. Even though I had experienced a very dramatic encounter with God in 1976, I was beginning to notice that my once enthusiastic faith was quickly diminishing. In my struggle to renew that excitement, I considered all of the reasons that could be causing this dry spiritual period. I concluded that my daily discipline of praying and Bible reading had dwindled to only a few minutes of glancing at one or two passages and praying the same quick prayer.

At that point in my life, I attended a convention for youth workers where the topic of prayer was threaded through each speech, sermon, and testimony. Even Bible verses about prayer, such as James 4:2, "You do not have, because you do not ask God," were quoted repeatedly. Over a four-day period, I became deeply aware of the *prayerlessness* in my own life. Oh, I had always considered prayer a necessary and important spiritual discipline, but I secretly thought it was a rather dull part of one's spiritual life, and specifically for the elderly, or for those who had a lot of extra time. In fact, I even avoided seminars or books on the subject of prayer, believing that it was too boring and serious of a subject for me.

But at that convention, my interest was piqued when prayer was spoken of as the most exciting, adventurous aspect of one's spiritual life. As if I were hearing about prayer for the first time, I suddenly understood what was missing in my life!

By neglecting to pray, I was actually avoiding God! No wonder I had lost my enthusiasm!

In the last session of the convention, I made a radical decision—to spend one hour a day with God *for the rest of my life!* In order to keep accountable to that commitment, I placed a daily appointment with God on my calendar, until it became a habit.

After a few months, I began to look for ways to make my time with God more effective and better organized. One morning, I simply asked God for an idea to help me. Within minutes I began to write down the outline of *My Partner Prayer Notebook* (now in this journal format).

I divided my prayer time into "My Part" and "God's Part" and included the necessary ingredients to keep my relationship with God exciting, fresh, and growing stronger on a daily basis. I also included a section for recording any thoughts and "to-do's" that came to my mind during this time.

The first four sections are to record "My Part" in prayer:

P for prayers of PRAISE,
A for prayers of ADMISSION of sin,
R for prayers of REQUEST, and
T for prayers of THANKS to God.

The next five sections are for recording God's daily input to me through L–M–N–O–P.

L for LISTENING,
M for MESSAGES,
N for NEW TESTAMENT,
O for OLD TESTAMENT, and
P for PROVERBS.

PRAISE

I will praise you, O Lord, with all my heart; I will tell of all your wonders. I will be glad and rejoice in you; I will sing praise to your name, O Most High. Psalm 9:1–2

When you praise God, you can find yourself overwhelmed with His unfailing love and goodness! This PRAISE section is designed for expressing your praise to God for *who He is*, rather than for the things He *does*. (The THANKS section is the place to respond to God's blessings in your life with expressions of gratitude).

PRAISE becomes the…

Purposeful
Reverence and
Awe of God's
Integrity and
Sovereignty
Eternally!

By beginning your appointment with God each day in praise for who He is, you will be reminded of how big He is, how much He loves you, how awesome His creation is, and how forgiving He is. As you praise Him, you will find yourself easily saying, "I love You, Lord."

When you start your day in praise for the God of the universe, who holds the whole world—and you—in His hands, your anxieties and fears will begin to release!

Psalms is full of praise prayers to God. In reading and rereading Psalms, you have the opportunity to observe those who loved the Lord and how they intimately communicated to Him.

As you praise God, reflect on His righteousness, forgiveness, and mercy. Make this section a record of your personal praise prayers to God.

TRY IT! APPLY IT!

May my lips overflow with praise. Psalm 119:171

Imagine yourself a poet, songwriter, or painter, expressing your feelings to God in your own special way. That may seem awkward at first, but be creative! Write a poem or a song that focuses on God as your Creator, Friend, Redeemer, Father or King! Perhaps you are better at acrostics. Take the letters from A to Z and choose a word that best describes how you feel about God with each letter. For example: Awesome, Beautiful, Caring, etc.

You may have a favorite chorus you can sing or write down as you begin your time in the PRAISE section. Perhaps you can write an original song using words from Scripture. Often the lyrics of a hymn will express your heart of praise to God. Write the verses down, singing along as you go!

My favorite way to praise God is to go through the book of Psalms in numerical order, reading three or four psalms each day and writing out the verses that particularly reflect my own thoughts and feelings toward God. It seems as if God knows where I will be reading because each day I read verses that express exactly how I feel. Over the months and years, I have observed through the Psalms how the psalmists freely expressed their love toward God. It has both taught and encouraged me to do the same! And by monthly going through the entire book of Psalms, I am assured and reassured that God desires to meet *my* needs, hear *my* prayers, and protect *me* from all harm. My words of praise have grown more and more meaningful each day.

There is no more appropriate way to begin your time with God than in praise to Him.

ADMIT

Search me, O God, and know my heart; test me and know my anxious thoughts. See if there is any offensive way in me, and lead me in the way everlasting. Psalm 139:23–24

To admit that we sin is sometimes uncomfortable and can create a lot of tension within us. Yet according to 1 John 1:10, if we say we do not sin, we make God out to be a liar!

When we come to God, part of our confession to Him is that we *have* sinned and fallen short of the glory of God (Romans 3:23). It is this initial confession that so often releases stored-up guilt and heavy burdens and opens the door to His forgiveness (1 John 1:9).

Whenever I doubt that God forgives me or even wants to forgive me for my sins, I reflect on the day that I asked Him to come into my life, just as I was . . . broken, addicted, lost. The moment I confessed all of those shortcomings to Him, I felt released from the guilt and shame, and I knew He had forgiven me.

When I am not *feeling* forgiven, I think back to that day and claim 1 John 1:9 as my promise of His forgiveness. This practice gives me courage and hope to move on.

Sometimes, as we grow in our relationship with God, our tendency is to avoid confessing sin on a daily basis. Perhaps we are too busy and forget, or we may put it off until we have time to really work it out. Quite often, we just don't want to recognize or admit that we are separating ourselves from God and others by holding grudges, repeatedly blowing up with uncontrolled anger, or hanging on to bad attitudes and habits.

The continual struggle in understanding the broad scope of sin is that our society encourages us to walk in opposite ways from what the Bible teaches. But being in a right relationship with *God and others* includes owning up to our mistakes and shortcomings. Confessing our faults and disappointments to God *each day* makes it hard for those comfortable sins (such as jealousy, gossip and anger) to take hold and become habits in our lives. Avoiding the truth, or covering up our sins to spare ourselves from embarrassment, can lead to worse problems, add even more distance in our relationships, or even cause physical problems.

TRY IT! APPLY IT!

In the ADMIT section, you may want to begin by writing out Psalm 139:23, 24 (on opposite page), or similar verses that relate to admitting sin on a daily basis. An additional bonus to writing out a Scripture verse several days in a row is that you will have it memorized in a short time!

Sit quietly and wait for the Holy Spirit to bring to mind the times and ways in your day when you "blew it," missed the mark, or fell short. Then journal your thoughts and confessions, perhaps even abbreviating certain words you don't want anyone but God to know about! There will be times when your list is quite lengthy, but use those days as an incentive for improvement! Maybe even choose *one* item on your list to work on that day.

During the ADMIT time, you may find yourself feeling truly sorry, even crying. It is a humbling experience when you realize that you have hurt God and others by such things as selfishness and lack of self-control. Even prayer-lessness—or neglecting God—can be a cause for confession!

Unless you admit your sins, your actions will not change. Being sorry without being willing to *turn* from sin is not genuine repentance. True repentance leads to a changed mind and, ultimately, changed actions. Be honest with God—and yourself!

At the end of this ADMIT section, make a point of sincerely asking God to cleanse and forgive you of these sins and "make you new." Each day, ask Him to fill you with His Holy Spirit and renew your mind (Romans 12:2). You may choose to end this section with Psalm 119:133: "Direct my footsteps according to your word; let no sin rule over me."

Finally, *leave uplifted!* God loves you. It is His nature to forgive those who turn from sin and run to Him.

REQUEST

Ask and it will be given to you; seek and you will find; knock and the door will be opened to you. For everyone who asks receives; he who seeks finds; and to him who knocks, the door will be opened. Matthew 7:7–8

There are a number of verses in the Bible, like Matthew 7:7–8, that encourage you to ask God for His plan and will for your life. Philippians 4:6 invites you to pray about everything, rather than to worry. And Matthew 6:31–34 describes how many of us worry about things like clothes, food and drink, but in verse 33, we are reminded to " . . . seek first his kingdom and his righteousness, and all these things will be given to you as well."

What does it mean to "seek God first?" It means to look, search for, and pursue Him and His will for your life. And what better way to search for His will than through a daily conversation with Him?

God wants us to ask Him for His will. In James 4:2 we read, "You do not have, because you do not ask God." Wow! The goal of this section is to provide a written record of your requests made to God, as well as a place to record the results. You will be amazed to see how specifically God answers your prayers!

When I am praying about my hopes and dreams, Psalm 37:4 comes to mind: "Delight yourself in the Lord and he will give you the desires of your heart." Take a moment to think about what it means for you to "delight yourself in the Lord."

I am absolutely convinced that God wants to bless your life through answered prayer. He desires to meet your every need (Philippians 4:19) and give you direction for a fulfilling life (Proverbs 3:5, 6).

If you want to know God's perfect will for your life, you must *ask* Him for it. Remember, once you ask Him, you must be willing to wait for His timing, trust that He has it all in control, and obey what you believe He has told you. (If "knowing God's will" is something you are unsure of, be sure to take extra time to study that subject.)

TRY IT! APPLY IT!

The REQUEST section is where you talk to God about all of *your* needs, desires, and dreams; you'll need another page to talk to Him about your family and friends, as well as *world* needs (such as homeless people, missing children, politicians, etc.).

In order to be diligent in praying for those who have asked for your prayers and for those you want to pray for daily, begin a prayer REQUEST list in the section reserved in the back of the journal. Refer to it, and revise it daily, but do not feel as if you have to rewrite the list each day. Make your list as detailed or general as fits your personality. I personally list all family members by name and include a little phrase by each of their names.

Next, you might list projects and plans for which you are seeking God's guidance. A section for those who are in need of physical or emotional healing may be appropriate for your prayer list. Others to include on your list would be government leaders who need safety, protection, and wisdom from God. Remember to pray for those who are helping to meet the needs of the physically and spiritually needy. Add the names of leaders and persons who touch your life. You will be amazed to see how your heart grows in concern and love for others as you pray daily for them.

After you have prayed through your daily prayer list, ask God to direct your day—your plans, your work, your steps. (I don't recopy my list each day, *but I do leave space to add to it.*) Each day, add any new situations that need God's intervention.

Another idea is to pray Scripture verses. For example, Colossians 1:9–12 is an *excellent* passage to turn into a prayer for yourself and others on a daily basis.

I firmly believe that God *wants* us to *ask* Him for His direction for our lives—now and for the future. James 4:2 says, "You do not have because you do not ask God." It is very exciting—and faith building—to watch God *answer* your prayers, especially when you have been diligent to ask Him for His will and have waited for His answer! (God *always* answers the prayers of His children, but it may not always be with a "Yes." "No" and "Wait" are answers, too!) You have really begun to trust in Him when you are open to His answer and timing for your requests. Now you try it, and in faith, expect results!

Morning by morning, O Lord, you hear my voice; morning by morning I lay my requests before you and wait in expectation. Psalm 5:3

THANKS

Be joyful always; pray continually; give thanks in all circumstances, for this is God's will for you in Christ Jesus. 1 Thessalonians 5:16–18

This section is the place, each day, where you can record and rejoice in answers to prayer. Here, you can express appreciation to God for His goodness, mercy and blessings toward you.

God is intimately concerned with every detail of your life. When you acknowledge to yourself and others that He is working in your life and that He deserves the credit for your accomplishments and talents, a written thank-you note then becomes a genuine expression of your gratitude toward Him. Thanking God replaces taking personal credit for good deeds done! In addition, there is no longer credibility given to chance or luck.

When you see God as the source of all your blessings, you will have a heart *full* of prayers to thank Him!

TRY IT! APPLY IT!

This section is a breeze! How would you thank a friend or family member in a thank-you note? You would probably include sincere appreciation for specific gifts or treats or good deeds.

Therefore, each day, take a moment to think through your current or past day. How has God specifically touched your life or encouraged you? Write a thank-you note to Him! You may even want to create a poem that expresses the words in your heart.

LISTENING

The Lord confides in those who fear him; he makes his covenant known to them. Psalm 25:14

The spiritual discipline of *listening to God* is one of continual struggle for all Christians. It takes practice to hear God's voice! In fact, younger Christians may not feel confident in pursuing this section, but wise and godly counsel from a pastor or parent, and the direction found in the Word of God, will encourage you in the practice of *listening to God.*

This section can be most difficult because you may question whether *God* is speaking to you. You may wonder if the thoughts you are thinking are simply your own.

Even though some doubt may exist, quiet yourself before the Lord and record what you feel He is saying to you. "Be still, and know that I am God" (Psalm 46:10).

Listening to the voice of God is not meant to be magical or mystical. Hearing God's voice in the midst of busy lives, emotional pain, or even temptation comes with practice and takes discernment. But if you are regularly reading the Bible, it won't be long before you begin to know the Shepherd's voice (John 10:4).

I have found that I am most ready to hear God's voice when I purposely find a quiet place to read the Bible and then think about the verses I've just read. In those moments, I ask God to reveal His thoughts and plans to me, and then I wait to hear His voice. I usually underline or highlight a few of the verses that relate to my life situations.

You may also hear God's voice as He uses others—Christian friends, pastors, speakers, or books—to prompt your thinking, actions and emotions. If you are struggling with this section, simply ask God to help you hear His voice.

TRY IT! APPLY IT!

Begin this section with a silent or written prayer, asking God to speak to you by His Holy Spirit. Be specific in asking about your needs and decisions, and ask if He has any direction for you. Be silent and attentive to the next thoughts that cross your mind.

Many times a Scripture verse will come to mind. Write the verse down in this section. Then look up the reference and read the entire paragraph or chapter for any further insight or inspiration that it might give to you. Notice the verses that have direct implication or application to the prayers you have previously prayed in your PRAISE, ADMIT, REQUESTS, and THANKS sections.

Very often I am encouraged, comforted, corrected, or directed by what has come to mind and what I have read. Once, concerned about an upcoming move, the passage in John 14 about God's peace came to my mind. I had been somewhat anxious about where we were going to live. When I came to verse 2, "I am going there to prepare a place for you," my heart jumped with excitement and I wrote the verse down in my LISTENING section. That afternoon, a gentleman, whom I had never met, called and asked if our family would house-sit for him for three months!

On another occasion, I felt that God was telling me to "watch my driving." I wrote the phrase down in my LISTENING section . . . and two hours later I got a sixty-dollar speeding ticket. I have taken my LISTENING section more seriously from that moment on! And I haven't gotten any more speeding tickets!

Many times in my LISTENING section I have received *hope* through the Word of God. Every day, I wait and watch and ask God for words of encouragement and direction in my life—and every day they come!

God might call you by name or speak to you about doing something for someone. You may feel led to pray for another person whose need He brings to your mind.

The more time you spend listening to God, the easier it will become to hear Him and recognize His voice. You may want to begin with only a few minutes of silent listening and then allow your time with Him to gradually increase. Write down what you feel He is saying to you.

MESSAGES

*Remember your leaders, who spoke the word of God to you. Consider the
outcome of their way of life and imitate their faith.* Hebrews 13:7

In *My Partner Prayer Journal* you can include any and all notes from the
teachings and/or sermons that you hear. Take this journal with you whenever
you go to church, Sunday school, or retreats, or when you are listening to an
audiotape or radio teaching. Always date each page and make a note of the
teacher, leader, or conference speaker. This will bring back to you the memory
and significance of God working in your life.

As God speaks to you through other people, write down the challenges
they give and make a note of the Scripture references they quote. God will use
these people and your notes to increase your knowledge of Him. By writing
down or taking notes of what you hear, you won't forget them and will be able
to share them with other family members and friends.

NEW TESTAMENT

The whole Bible was given to us by inspiration from God and is useful to teach us what is true and to make us realize what is wrong in our lives; it straightens us out and helps us do what is right. 2 Timothy 3:16 (TLB)

If you have not yet read through the New Testament chapter by chapter, do so! If you have, you should seek the advice of your pastor, youth director, parent, or Christian bookstore regarding the many ways you can study the Bible.

The most effective tool I have used for over fifteen years is a Bible divided into 365 days. In 1998 I designed a special edition of this Bible to be used with *My Partner Prayer Journal* called the *Change Your Life Daily Bible**. It is the entire Bible organized in 365 daily readings, giving you a planned reading schedule of the New Testament, Old Testament, Proverbs, and Psalms. (You can read through the Bible in two years by reading the New Testament only the first year, and the Old Testament in the second year.)

I would encourage you to read the Bible every day and to take notes on what you read and how it applies to you. Underline, highlight, and date verses that touch your heart, correcting or comforting you.

The New Testament begins with four books called the Gospels: Matthew, Mark, Luke and John. They detail the life and work of Christ on earth. The remaining books of the New Testament are letters written to believers in Christ, to build them up and encourage their faith. Though they are almost two thousand years old, they apply to followers of Christ today just as much as they did to the people to whom they were written.

*(The *Change Your Life Daily Bible* is available through Becky Tirabassi Change Your Life®, Inc.)

TRY IT! APPLY IT!

Pray about your time in God's Word—where to read, what study guide to use, and how to make Bible reading a priority in your life. As you read the Bible on a daily basis, jot down the verses that stand out and cause you to reflect on issues and concerns in your life.

Make note of the verses that challenge, encourage or comfort you. Compile a list of those verses in the back of your notebook or Bible under designated topics. You may choose to use a highlighter to emphasize verses or paragraphs that speak to you in a special way. Note the date and place when you hear a message on a particular New Testament passage. This practice will remind you of God's message for your life that day—and encourage you at a later date! Don't hesitate to ask questions. Ask God for understanding (John 14).

OLD TESTAMENT

I have hidden your word in my heart that I might not sin against you.
Psalm 119:11

The Old Testament is the Word of God written prior to the coming of Christ, the promised Messiah. It is broken down into books of History, Law, Poetry, and Prophets. These books tell us many stories of God's love, forgiveness, direction, and provision for His people, Israel. As with all stories, they are told so the reader can relate to the spiritual concepts through the use of analogies, parables, and prophecies.

The Old Testament overflows with messages and meaning for the believer today and presents the facts of our faith as rooted in history. In addition to affirming our faith, Psalm 119:165 says, "Great peace have they who love your law, and nothing can make them stumble." The promises of the Old Testament reach deep into the believer's heart, filling him or her with the hope of God.

Over and over I experience increased faith and hope as I read the Old Testament. Contrary to those who claim that the Old Testament is outdated, or irrelevant for today, I have found it to deepen my knowledge of God and strengthen my hope and confidence in Him.

TRY IT! APPLY IT!

I rejoice in following your statues as one rejoices in great riches. I medi-tate on your precepts and consider your ways. I delight in your decrees; I will not neglect your word. Psalm 119:14–16

Don't be fooled by the word *old!* The Lord's mercies are new every morn-ing, and so is the freshness of His Word!

Seek guidance on where you should read in the Old Testament, if you are hesitant. There are many daily guides, commentaries, devotionals, topical sys-tems, and study guides to help you. I would encourage you to read through the entire Old Testament on a regular basis.

The *Change Your Life Daily Bible* organizes the Bible into 365 daily read-ings, so that it is easy to read through the entire Bible in a year. Each day's reading includes passages from the Old Testament, New Testament, Psalms, and Proverbs.

Read your Bible a lot or a little at a time—whatever you think you can keep up with. Stay at it. If you've stopped reading your Bible, pick it back up, or change the methods that you were previously using. At all costs, stay in the Word of God—it is God's voice to you. It is your lifeline! Therefore, I encour-age you to plan time each day to read the Bible.

Love the Lord your God with all your heart and with all your soul and with all your strength. Deuteronomy 6:5

If you need a push, read a psalm every day!

PROVERBS

These are the proverbs of King Solomon of Israel, David's son: He wrote them to teach his people how to live—how to act in every circumstance, for he wanted them to be understanding, just and fair in everything they did. "I want to make the simple-minded wise!" he said. "I want to warn young men about some problems they will face. I want those already wise to become the wiser and become leaders by exploring the depths of meaning in these nuggets of truth." Proverbs 1:1–6 (TLB)

Look more closely at the verses above. The book of Proverbs is for everyone! Who has not been tempted to gossip, go with the crowd, or follow the lust in his or her heart? I know I have been!

That is why Proverbs is so practical. It offers the solid advice you need to make right decisions in a world whose ways are opposite of God's ways.

Proverbs is not outdated. With its warnings and advice, it cuts to the core of your conscience at times. You'll also notice that Proverbs is for people of all ages and stages, and advises us how to make right choices. It provides all generations with wise and practical counsel.

If you read one chapter of Proverbs a day, on most months you will finish all thirty-one chapters. Your hunger for the Bible will grow, and God's Spirit will teach you wisdom and godliness.

TRY IT! APPLY IT!

Read the proverb found in the *Change Your Life Daily Bible* or a verse of your choice—if not an entire chapter—each day. In this section, jot down any thoughts that come to mind as you read the Proverbs.

As you read, ask yourself:

Is God using His Word to challenge me?

Do shortcomings in my life come to mind as I read?

Write those thoughts down in this section. Then, you might want to write a message to God, asking Him to give you wisdom or strength in those areas.

I would encourage you to memorize proverbs that seem particularly pertinent to you. Write them out in this section of your notebook. It might also help to write a proverb on a three-by-five-inch card and carry it with you so you can recite it several times during the day.

TO DO

Teach us to number our days aright, that we may gain a heart of wisdom.
Psalm 90:12

To do, or not to do, that is the question.

Most of us tend to put off 'til tomorrow anything that makes us uncomfortable or looks hard. How do you overcome bad habits and win over laziness? Prayer and effort seem to be the only ways! Scores of good books and tapes on time management are available to encourage you and exhort you in the area of discipline with time and talents. Finding your weaknesses and tackling them head-on is another key. But most experts agree that writing down, making lists, numbering priorities, and keeping a calendar will help you become more organized and get more done. More importantly, you will get the *right* things done more often.

How we spend our time makes a great deal of difference in what we will accomplish in our personal and professional lives, as well as in our spiritual lives.

GUIDELINES

The following guidelines are suggestions to help you get a smooth start as you "talk to God" and "listen to God" in *My Partner Prayer Journal*.

1. Think of your journal as your daily partner. Take it with you to church, retreats, vacations, and study groups; use it as a datebook/daily organizer. Put it in a familiar place each day, so it will be readily available when you need it and are looking for it.

2. Picture yourself in an actual appointment with God. Choose a quiet spot and, most importantly, *plan* for this time. You may have to set your alarm for earlier than usual, carving out additional time rather than squeezing time already allotted for other things. You may actually want to block time out on your daily calendar to keep from changing and shifting your quiet time. Sometimes you will have to plan around other people's schedules to assure yourself of few (or no) interruptions. Have an attitude of expectancy (Psalm 5:3).

3. Choose the same time of day for your appointment whenever possible. This habit becomes a link to consistency. The times you have already set for regular responsibilities, such as leaving for school or work, may need to be adjusted or rearranged. This will enable you to spend quality, unrushed time praying and reading your Bible.

4. Decide upon a specific amount of time that you will spend in prayer and Bible study. This time can be lengthened or shortened once you have determined what is realistic for your life. A minimum of twenty minutes is a good place to begin. You can set this amount of time after reviewing your current weekly schedule and praying about how much time is appropriate for you to spend having a quiet time. Share your goal with a friend, parent, pastor or prayer partner. He or she can help keep you accountable to your decision. I'm *convinced* that this guideline of a specific length of time has made my own daily quiet time a success. I actually note the time when I first put my pencil to the paper to help make sure that I fulfill my commitment to have an appointment with God. There have been *numerous* times when I would have slept in, changed plans, or been too tired to have my quiet time had I not made this decision. It has turned into a positive action step, rather than a burden hanging over me.

5. If you have an interruption, return to your appointment with God at the earliest possible time. When I have too many interruptions, I know I've been planning poorly, procrastinating, oversleeping, or that my priorities are out of balance. I'm convinced that the earlier in the day that I set my daily appointment with God, the better my day will begin and end.

6. If you miss a day, or even a week, immediately start up again—as often as you have to until your time with God becomes a daily habit. Don't try to catch up or double up what you think you have missed. Just press on! Persist. Don't give up! You can do it! You need it! Remind yourself of Hebrews 12:11: "No discipline seems pleasant at the time, but painful. Later on, however, it produces a harvest of righteousness and peace for those who have been trained by it." Dating each page will help you remain accountable to yourself, as well as to chart your personal spiritual journey.

7. Make your time with God a priority. *Plan for it!* And expect great things!

PERSONAL COMMENTS

Since 1984 I have become convinced that writing one's prayers in an organized, accountable, and relational system is truly the key to having a daily conversation with God. Every concern, hope, confession, request, or *thank you* that I have expressed to God in writing has been a record of my spiritual journey.

Written prayer has proven to me:

- that God answers specific prayer requests,
- that one can grow a heart for His Word as it is the source of His answers,
- that anyone can become a "listener" to God—through practice and experience, and
- that every dream and desire of your heart that you express to God will in His time be answered in His way—beyond what you could imagine, even when the answer is no.

My hope would be that *My Partner Prayer Journal* and its companions, *Let Prayer Change Your Life* and *Let Prayer Change Your Life Workbook*, and the *Change Your Life Daily Bible* will become encouraging, life-changing resources for you.

If you would like to order additional journals, please use the order form in this journal or contact your bookstore.

In addition, if you would be interested in hosting a motivational Change Your Life® seminar, or would desire companion resources to this notebook, please contact Becky Tirabassi Change Your Life®, Inc. for further information.

Sincerely,
Becky Tirabassi

Becky Tirabassi Change Your Life®, Inc.
Box 9672, Newport Beach, California 92660
1-800-444-6189
www.changeyourlifedaily.com

PUTTING IT TOGETHER

The following is a description and a sample of my two-way conversation with God today using the pattern of PART for "my part" in prayer, and LMNOP as God's part in prayer. I used the CYL Daily Bible as my resource for listening to God's voice.

I begin my time in prayer with **Praise**, paraphrasing one or more Psalms each day, acknowledging His power and presence in my life and the world.

I proceed to **Admit** my sins in writing after beginning with Psalm 139:23, 24.

When I arrive at the **Request** section, I have reserved four pages in the back of MPPJ to record an on-going prayer request list. I review the request list *daily*, adding to and revising it as necessary. For continuity, I will write a specific request in today's date.

I continue on with the pattern of PART by writing a note of **Thanks** to God for something He has done for me.

I proceed to **Listen** to God by recording any thoughts or impressions.

Note: Because today is a weekday, I have not included a Message on this day's journal entry. But on Sunday I always take notes of the sermon, so with the MPPJ, I would date the top of the first fresh page in the journal, title the sermon, and record the name of the speaker. My notes would follow . . .

Finally, I use the *Change Your Life Daily Bible* as the tool to help me *daily listen* to God's voice. It is divided into 365 readings of Old Testament, New Testament, Proverbs, and Psalms. I record the verses in each section that stand out, arouse my emotions to change something in my life, or cause me to follow a certain direction.

The **To Do** section is the last place of response. Peter Marshall said that prayer is where we "get our marching orders from the Captain." I record any action steps, ideas, or practical "to do's" that come to my mind during this time of prayer. In addition, I might transfer them to a separate calendar at this time.

TODAY

Praise

Psalm 54 (my paraphrase) . . . *O God, save me by Your name. Vindicate me by Your might. Hear my prayer and listen to the words of my mouth.*

Surely You are my help. I will sacrifice a freewill offering to You and praise Your name for You are good. You have delivered me . . . and I will look in triumph on my foes.

ADMIT

Search me, O God (Psalm 139:23–24) and know my heart; test me and know my anxious thoughts; see the offensive ways in me . . . and lead me in Your way . . . please. Yes Lord, lead me in Your ways . . . not mine. Give me more of You. Cause me to want more of You and less of me. Give me courage to abstain from doubt and fear just as You have given me the courage to abstain from alcohol and anger. Cleanse, renew, and change me today.

REQUEST

Lord, continue to put the pieces together for Jake (my son). As he pursues the desires of his heart, thank you for so many people and opportunities you allowed to fall into place for over the past few weeks. Continue to give Him faith-filled friends, a heart after you and orchestrate—soon—the place where you would have him to live for the next year.

THANKS

O Lord, thank you so much for the job opportunity that You brought into Jake's life this week! It seems just perfect for him—in every way! We (Roger and I) are so very, very grateful that You provided something that so wonderfully fits his personality, gifts, and passions. Thank You so much . . .

(As I listen to God, I recorded these words as I read the Daily Bible and meditated on God's Word . . .)

Miss Becky (I always start with this affectionate phrase),
My salvation is at hand. I have shown you what is good. I have shown you the end from the beginning. Do not fear for I am with you. Do not anxiously look about you, for I am your God. Surely I will help you. Surely I will uphold you with My righteous right hand.
I love you . . .

The goal of *My Partner Prayer Journal* is to record your spiritual journey through your conversations with God during the next sixty to ninety days. When you have filled this journal, don't let that stop you from daily recording your conversations with God. Be sure to keep extra journals on hand, and be encouraged to keep all of them in a safe place for the rest of your life!

- Fasting
- 30 day   9/28 → 10/28
- No cola
→ New Job → GS-13, Less stress, Less Travel

REQUEST LIST

REQUEST LIST

REQUEST LIST

REQUEST LIST

THANK YOU

In 1984 I wrote . . . There are so many family members and friends who have made this quiet-time organizer possible. I would like to thank each of them for their love, patience, inspiration, motivation, capital, encouragement, and so much more.

Jesus . . . for the idea!
Roger and Jacob, my wonderful husband and son
Mom, Dad, and Rick Hunter for believing in me
My sister and brother-in-law, Reg and Dick Mantei
Steve and Cheryl Johnson for MUCH
The Berea High Campus Life kids and cheerleaders
The LeFebvre family for their Digital and their time
The Puls families
Gregg Lewis for encouragement
The Menefees
My prayer partners (for consistent prayer!)
Dr. Schuller for encouraging people to ask God for an idea
And for the all-nighter that got this going!
(Thanks Stephanie and Sherry...)

In 2003 I am still encouraged by the many friends who have challenged me to sustain the discipline of daily prayer and regular fasting. They are:

Dr. Bill and Vonette Bright
Thomas Nelson Publishers
Women of Faith Friends
And the C4L Prayer Partners.

When I designed this journal in 1984, I never dreamed more than 250,000 men, women, and students would find *My Partner* to be their companion to "talk to God" and "listen to God."

Thanks to each of you!
Becky

ABOUT THE AUTHOR

Becky Tirabassi is a renowned motivational speaker and bestselling author of *Change Your Life, Let Prayer Change Your Life, Let Faith Change Your Life,* and numerous other books. A guest contributor on *The CBS Early Show* in 2001, Becky appears regularly on television and radio, inspiring audiences across the country to change their lives for the better. She has appeared on *Fox and Friends, Focus on the Family,* and several other national programs. She is the president and founder of Becky Tirabassi Change Your Life®, Inc., a multimedia company. She also maintains an extensive national speaking tour.

ORDER FORM

Qty	Item	ISBN	Cost Each	Total
	Let Prayer Change Your Life	0-7852-6885-5	10.99	
	My Partner Prayer Journal	0-7852-6382-9	16.99	
	Refills for My Partner Prayer Journal	0-7852-7482-0	10.99	
	Change Your Life Daily Bible	0-8423-3289-8	20.00	
	Let Prayer Change Your Life Workbook	0-7852-6658-5	19.99	
	Let Faith Change Your Life	0-7852-7235-6	17.99	
	Let Love Change Your Life	0-7852-6509-0	14.99	
			Subtotal	
	California residents add 7.75% sales tax			
			Subtotal	
	Add $2.50 postage for each product ordered			
	Handling Charge			
			TOTAL	